AF228555

WASHINGTON WIZARDS

BY ANTHONY K. HEWSON

SportsZone

An Imprint of Abdo Publishing
abdobooks.com

abdobooks.com

Published by Abdo Publishing, a division of ABDO, PO Box 398166, Minneapolis, Minnesota 55439. Copyright © 2023 by Abdo Consulting Group, Inc. International copyrights reserved in all countries. No part of this book may be reproduced in any form without written permission from the publisher. SportsZone™ is a trademark and logo of Abdo Publishing.

Printed in China.
052022
092022

Cover Photo: Christian Peterson/Getty Images Sport/Getty Images
Interior Photos: Melinda Nagy/Shutterstock Images, 1; Focus on Sport/Getty Images Sport/Getty Images, 4, 7, 8, 13, 15, 32, 35, 37; AP Images, 9; Bettmann/Getty Images, 10; Brian Kersey/AP Images, 19; Mark Goldman/Icon Sportswire/Getty Images, 21; Alex Goodlett/Getty Images Sport/Getty Images, 22; Focus on Sport/Getty Images, 24; Jonathan Daniel/Getty Images Sport/Getty Images, 28; Nick Wass/AP Images, 30; Scott Taetsch/Getty Images Sport/Getty Images, 31; Jeff Roberson/AP Images, 38; Rob Carr/ Getty Images Sport/Getty Images, 40

Editor: Charlie Beattie
Series Designer: Joshua Olson

Library of Congress Control Number: 2021951668

Publisher's Cataloging-in-Publication Data

Names: Hewson, Anthony K., author.
Title: Washington Wizards / by Anthony K. Hewson
Description: Minneapolis, Minnesota : Abdo Publishing, 2023 | Series: Inside the NBA | Includes online resources and index.
Identifiers: ISBN 9781532198472 (lib. bdg.) | ISBN 9781098272128 (ebook)
Subjects: LCSH: Washington Wizards (Basketball team)--Juvenile literature. | Basketball--Juvenile literature. | Professional sports--Juvenile literature. | Sports franchises--Juvenile literature.
Classification: DDC 796.32364--dc23

TABLE OF CONTENTS

CHAPTER ONE

GREAT IN '78

The Washington Bullets could see their dream slipping away in Game 7 of the 1978 National Basketball Association (NBA) Finals. Washington had led by as many as 13 points in the fourth quarter. But with 90 seconds to play, the Seattle SuperSonics trailed them by only four. The next minute and a half would determine the NBA champion.

The Bullets were an unlikely finalist in 1978. Washington had barely finished above .500 at 44–38. It was the team's worst record in six seasons. But the Bullets believed in themselves. They were still loaded with talent. Superstar center Wes Unseld was getting older, but he was still the team leader. Power forward Elvin Hayes, known as "the Big E," was a regular All-Star. Small forward Bobby Dandridge was a scoring threat.

The Bullets had already taken their fans on an amazing playoff ride. After knocking off the Atlanta Hawks 2–0 in a

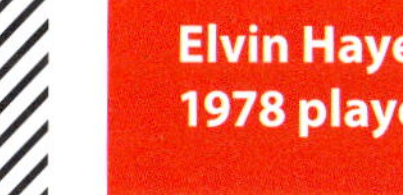

Elvin Hayes's, *left*, defensive effort was key for Washington during the 1978 playoffs.

best-of-three series, they upset the San Antonio Spurs. They then scored an even bigger upset in the conference finals against superstar forward Julius Erving and the Philadelphia 76ers.

FANTASTIC FINALS

The Finals went back and forth with the two teams alternating victories. After Seattle went up 3–2, the Sonics had a chance to close it out on the Bullets' home court. But backed by more than 19,000 of their fans, the Bullets blew out Seattle 117–82 to force Game 7.

The Bullets felt the pressure to win the game. In the locker room beforehand, both Hayes and Unseld spoke to the team. They remembered how it felt to lose in the Finals. And at the age of 32, they didn't know how many more chances they might get.

"We said, 'We don't have four or five more years—we have to do this now,'" Hayes said. "I think the guys looked into their hearts and said, 'Let's do it.'"

Washington had a balanced team. That showed with a minute left to go in Game 7. Reserve forward Mitch Kupchak scooped up a loose ball under the offensive basket and

Forward Mitch Kupchak was one of many Bullets role players who stepped up during the team's 1978 postseason run.

laid it in. He was also fouled on the play. He made his free throw, pushing the lead back to seven points.

Seattle did not go away. The Sonics cut the lead to two points with 18 seconds left. With time running out, Seattle had to foul if it wanted to extend the game.

The Sonics chose to foul Unseld, who was not a great free-throw shooter. He made less than 54 percent of his foul shots that season. Earlier in Game 7, he had missed three in a row. But Unseld stepped up and calmly nailed both shots.

The Bullets relied on the veteran presence of center Wes Unseld, *right*, during the 1978 playoffs.

Seattle needed a quick basket. Guard Dennis Johnson pulled up for a jump shot that rattled in and out. Unseld nabbed his ninth rebound of the game. He spotted Dandridge streaking up the court and threw a perfect pass. Dandridge grabbed it, then soared in the air and dunked with two hands to cap off the game in style. The Washington Bullets were going to win their first NBA title.

As the horn sounded, the Bullets threw their arms up in celebration. They made a triumphant line as they streaked off the court to celebrate in the locker room. The fans started their own celebration back home in Washington. Unseld was named Most Valuable Player (MVP) of the Finals. He was finally a champion.

It was a true team victory. Dandridge and guard Charles Johnson led the way with 19 points. Six players scored in double digits. Hayes played only 30 minutes before fouling out,

Hayes poses with the trophy after the Bullets defeated the Seattle SuperSonics in Game 7 of the 1978 NBA Finals.

but he still scored 12 points. Afterward, he had an answer for any critics.

"They can say whatever they want," Hayes replied with a smile. "But they gotta say one thing: E's a world champion. He wears the ring."

CHAPTER TWO

CAPITAL BOUND

The story of the Washington Wizards began in 1961 in Chicago. After its founding in 1946, the NBA made the Chicago Packers one of its first expansion teams. But the Packers were one of the worst teams in the NBA. They did not generate much excitement. A name change the next year to the Zephyrs didn't make much of a difference. After going 43–117 in two seasons, the Zephyrs blew out of the Windy City and landed in Baltimore, Maryland.

The team then took on its third name in three years and became the Bullets. The name was already associated with success in Baltimore. An earlier team called the Bullets had been founded in 1944. They chose the name because it reflected their explosive talent and team speed.

The original Bullets won the 1948 Basketball Association of America title. That league changed its name to the NBA in 1949.

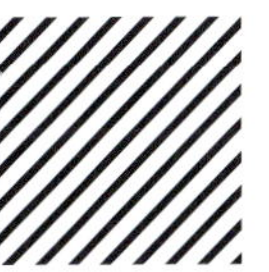

Walt Bellamy, *center*, of the Chicago Packers catches a pass against the St. Louis Hawks during a 1961 game.

After just seven full seasons, though, the Bullets shut down for good. The team stopped playing in November 1954, 14 games into the season. No NBA team has folded since.

The new Bullets began play in the fall of 1963. The Chicago years didn't produce many wins. But the team arrived in Baltimore with a pair of former Rookie of the Year winners. Center Walt Bellamy won the award in 1961–62, and small forward Terry Dischinger won in 1962–63. Both were key players during the first season in Baltimore.

In 1964 a group led by Baltimore businessman Abe Pollin bought the Bullets for $1.1 million. That was a record purchase price for an NBA team at the time. Pollin owned the team for the next 46 years.

Despite trading Dischinger before the 1964–65 season, Baltimore improved to 37–43. The Bullets made the playoffs for the first time. They even scored a first-round upset of the St. Louis Hawks before eventually losing to the Los Angeles Lakers.

Bellamy had led the team in scoring four years in a row. But he was traded in November 1965 to the New York Knicks. The Bullets had lost another superstar. But they still had a nicely balanced team that made it back to the playoffs.

DRAFTING A DYNASTY

At the 1967 NBA Draft, the Bullets grabbed a player who transformed the team. With the second pick, Baltimore selected guard Earl "the Pearl" Monroe. A record scorer in college, Monroe was known for his flashy moves on the court. He led the team in scoring in 1967–68 and won Rookie of the Year.

Another second overall draft pick in 1968 landed the Bullets center Wes Unseld. He became the greatest player in franchise history. Unseld was never a big scorer but was a force under the basket. He was a rebounding machine. And his passing ability led to many offensive chances for teammates.

Earl "the Pearl" Monroe (10) was one of the NBA's most exciting players in the 1960s and 1970s.

Unseld wasn't just Rookie of the Year in 1968–69. He was MVP as well. That year the Bullets won 57 games. In doing so, the team began a streak of 12 straight postseason appearances.

The Bullets were an offensive machine. The 1969–70 team averaged 120.7 points per game. That was the most in team history. But the New York Knicks were a constant playoff obstacle. New York knocked Baltimore out of the postseason for the second straight year.

The teams met again in the 1971 Eastern Conference finals. The Bullets had finished only 42–40 that season. But Monroe, Unseld, and power forward Gus Johnson stepped up in the playoffs. After a first-round upset of the Philadelphia 76ers, Baltimore was ready for New York. But the Knicks quickly went up 2–0 in the series. It looked like they would win again. However, the Bullets roared back to force Game 7. Then they knocked off the Knicks on their home court. Monroe's 26 points highlighted a memorable win.

The Bullets could not keep the run going in the NBA Finals. The Milwaukee Bucks swept Baltimore and took the title. But it was still Baltimore's deepest playoff run so far.

ON THE MOVE AGAIN

The Bullets won the Central Division every year from 1971 to 1975. But the franchise went through a lot of changes. Monroe was traded early in the 1971–72 season. Johnson was traded

Phil Chenier, *right,* played nine seasons with the Bullets and averaged 17.9 points per game.

after that season. Then the whole team left town in 1973. The Bullets relocated to the Washington, DC, area. After one season as the Capital Bullets, they officially became the Washington Bullets for 1974–75.

The 1974–75 season was a special one for the new Washingtonians. All-Stars Unseld, Elvin Hayes, and shooting guard Phil Chenier led the Bullets to a team-record 60 wins.

Washington then made it back to the NBA Finals too. This time they could not overcome the Golden State Warriors, however, losing in four straight games.

It was the surprising 1977–78 Bullets that finally delivered a championship. And they nearly pulled off a repeat in 1979. In a rematch with the Seattle SuperSonics, Washington won Game 1, only to lose the next four.

With Unseld and Hayes getting older, the Bullets' glory days were fading. By 1981 they were out of the playoffs for the first time in 13 years. Unseld retired that summer, and Hayes was traded. The Bullets struggled to replace their record-setting stars for the next 20 years.

Even without superstars, the Bullets were still a consistent playoff team in the 1980s. But postseason success was hard to come by. The Bullets failed to win a playoff series in five straight tries from 1984 to 1988. After going 42–40 in 1986–87, Washington did not have another winning record until 1997.

YOUNG WIZARDS

In the middle of many losing seasons, the Bullets started to assemble some new, young talent. Future All-Star forward Juwan Howard was drafted in 1994. Washington then swung a big trade on November 17, 1994. The Bullets traded three first-round draft picks and forward Tom Gugliotta for forward Chris Webber. Howard and Webber had been teammates on two University of Michigan teams that reached the Final Four.

Injuries limited Webber in his first few seasons. But he was healthy for 1996–97. He and Howard led the Bullets back to the playoffs. Washington's 44–38 record was its best since 1978–79. The team was swept by the reigning NBA champion Chicago Bulls, but fans felt Washington had a strong core of players for the future.

While the players may have been set, plenty of changes were coming to Washington. In 1995 Bullets owner Abe Pollin announced he intended to change the team's name. Pollin's friend, Israeli prime minister Yitzhak Rabin, had recently been assassinated. Washington also experienced a high amount of gun violence in the 1990s. For these reasons, Pollin felt that Bullets was no longer an appropriate name for a sports team.

The team asked fans to suggest new ideas. Out of 2,000 options, five finalists emerged: Dragons, Express, Stallions, Sea Dogs, and Wizards. The team set up a phone line for fans to call in and vote. In the spring of 1997, Wizards was announced as the winner.

That wasn't the only big change. After decades of playing 25 minutes away in the suburb of Landover, Maryland, the Wizards moved into a new downtown arena for the 1997–98 season. The team's colors were changed as well. No longer dressed in red, white, and blue, the Wizards now played in blue, gold, and black. Everything was set for a new era in Washington.

With Howard, Webber, and star point guard Rod Strickland, the Wizards made another try for the playoffs in 1997–98. They were edged out on the final day of the regular season, finishing 42–40. The same core didn't get a chance to try again in 1998–99 because Webber was traded. Two years later, in 2000–01, the Wizards won just 19 games. More big changes were in store. One of the biggest saw Howard leave as part of an eight-player trade during the season.

Michael Jordan played 142 games for the Wizards over the course of two seasons.

By now the biggest star in Washington was in the front office. Former Chicago Bulls great Michael Jordan had joined the Wizards as president of basketball operations. One of his jobs was to sign new players. In September 2001, Jordan made his biggest free agent signing yet: himself.

Once the game's most dominant player, Jordan had been retired for three years. He was 38 when he joined the Wizards for the 2001–02 season. Jordan showed the world he still had many of the skills that had made him an all-time great. But even his 22.9 points per game couldn't pull the Wizards into the playoffs. Jordan spent one more season in a Wizards uniform before retiring permanently.

THE BIG THREE

Another high-scoring guard joined the team in 2003. Gilbert Arenas had been a talented player for two seasons with Golden State. The Wizards were hoping he could improve even more. Arenas did, and he was an All-Star for the first time after the 2004–05 season.

That same year, Arenas led Washington back to the playoffs. He formed a "Big Three" with forward Antawn Jamison and guard Larry Hughes. Arenas hit a buzzer-beater to win Game 5 in the opening round against the Bulls. Hughes then led the way with 21 points as the Wizards closed out the series in Game 6. It was Washington's first playoff series win since 1982.

It was also the only playoff series win for Washington with Arenas on the roster. The team reached the postseason in each of the next three years. Every time it was stopped by LeBron James and the Cleveland Cavaliers. Legal trouble for Arenas and a trade of Jamison ended the run of the Big Three by 2010.

A new era of Wizards ownership began that same year. Pollin had died in 2009, and new owner Ted Leonsis took full control of the team. Leonsis already owned the National Hockey League's Washington Capitals. As the Wizards' owner, he set out to make some changes fans had been asking for.

Wizards guard Gilbert Arenas was one of the NBA's best scorers during his first four seasons in Washington.

The team uniforms were the first change. Leonsis brought back the old red, white, and blue color scheme. He also changed the uniform design to look like the old Bullets uniforms. Many fans also wished the Bullets name would return. Leonsis considered it, but Washington remained the Wizards.

Forward Rui Hachimura was one of the key young players who helped Washington return to the playoffs in 2021.

SHOOTING TOWARD THE FUTURE

Wearing the new uniform was a new star player, John Wall. The Wizards were lucky to get the point guard. They had just a one in 10 chance to get the first overall draft pick in 2010. But they got it and used it to select the former University of Kentucky star.

Wall was just the kind of playmaker the Wizards needed. It took a few years to surround him with talent. Wall and fellow guard Bradley Beal teamed up and led Washington back to the playoffs in 2013–14. In 2017 the Wizards won their first division title since 1979. After knocking out the Atlanta Hawks, Washington faced the Boston Celtics in the second round. Wall hit a game-winning three-pointer to win Game 6, but Boston closed out the series in Game 7.

Wall was traded just before the 2020–21 season. Washington started terribly without him. After 49 games, the Wizards had a 17–32 record. But Beal led a turnaround. He averaged 31.3 points per game, and the Wizards went on a 17–6 run to close the season and make the playoffs. With a young core that included Beal and center Rui Hachimura, fans hoped Washington was finally building toward a championship.

CHAPTER THREE

WIZARDS WINNERS

The Chicago Packers did not provide many memorable moments in their 18–62 inaugural season. But one bright spot was the play of the team's first-ever draft pick, center Walt Bellamy. In 1961 Bellamy was less than a year removed from helping Team USA capture gold at the Olympic Games in Rome, Italy.

In Chicago, Bellamy was a great scorer on offense and a fierce defender. He won Rookie of the Year in 1961–62 while averaging 31.6 points per game. Bellamy ranked among the top 10 in points and rebounds in NBA history when he retired in 1974.

Earl "the Pearl" Monroe was one of the most exciting players of his era. Monroe was drafted second overall in 1967. He played just four years with the Bullets but provided a lifetime of thrills. Fans couldn't take their eyes off his spin moves, fake

Wes Unseld spent his entire career with the Bullets, and his number 41 jersey was retired in 1981.

shots, and other fancy tricks. But Monroe wasn't just flash. His average of 23.7 points per game ranks among the highest in team history.

Gus Johnson was another must-see player for Baltimore. The forward was a force at both ends of the court. Johnson averaged a double-double for his career. He was a five-time All-Star in nine seasons with the Bullets. Johnson's No. 25 is one of five retired by the team.

THE CONTENDERS

Coaching the Bullets was personal for Gene Shue. The Baltimore native played for the Bullets during their first year in Maryland. He became head coach in 1966. After a few tough years, the team improved and played for an NBA title in 1971. When the Bullets left for the DC area in 1973, Shue opted to stay home. He did, however, return to coach the Bullets for a second time from 1980 to 1986. His 522 wins are by far the most in team history.

A big reason for Shue's turnaround of the Bullets was the arrival of Wes Unseld in 1968. The second overall pick in that year's draft won Rookie of the Year and MVP. Though short for a center at 6 feet, 7 inches, Unseld was a powerful scorer and rebounder.

The Bullets had never finished with a winning record before Unseld. They had 10 in his 12 seasons on the roster. He won

Finals MVP honors in leading the Bullets to their first NBA title in 1978. Right after retiring, Unseld joined the Washington front office and later became head coach.

Big man Elvin Hayes was the only person chosen ahead of Unseld in the 1968 draft. The two players wound up teammates in 1972 after a trade. The two big men made the Bullets a true title contender.

Unseld and Hayes had plenty of supporting help in their run to the 1978 title. Durable forward Greg Ballard missed only 13 games in eight seasons with Washington. Only Hayes and Unseld played more games for the franchise.

Father and Son

Washington basketball is the Unseld family business. After Wes Unseld played 13 years for Washington, he stayed on with the team in its front office and later as head coach. Unseld's son Wes Jr. grew up hanging out with his dad at the arena. He later followed Wes Sr. into coaching. Wes Unseld Jr. was named Wizards head coach in 2021.

The Bullets teams of the 1980s did not have many stars, but Jeff Malone was one of their most reliable players. Malone averaged more than 20 points per game each season from 1985–86 to 1989–90. He trailed only Hayes in all-time scoring when he left the team in 1990.

Juwan Howard, *right,* and Chris Webber played together for two years in college and four with the Bullets/Wizards.

NEW KIDS ON THE BLOCK

The 1990s Bullets rebuild was focused mostly around two players. Juwan Howard was the team's top draft pick in 1994.

The 6-foot-9-inch forward gave the Bullets the scoring punch they needed and was also a star rebounder.

The other half of this dynamic duo was Chris Webber. Like Howard, he was a star at the University of Michigan. The do-it-all forward had just won Rookie of the Year in Golden State when Washington picked him up in a 1994 trade. He could score, rebound, and play tough defense. Webber's only problem was staying healthy. In 1995–96 he played just 15 games.

As the Wizards tried to build another playoff contender in the 2000s, they found a true superstar in Gilbert Arenas. The point guard's first two seasons in Golden State had been solid. But he reached new levels upon signing with the Wizards in 2003. Arenas turned into one of the best scorers in the NBA. He averaged a career-best 29.3 points per game in 2005–06. Point guards had historically been pass-first players. But Arenas's scoring ability helped usher in a new era at the position.

Arenas was one corner of the Big Three that also included guard Larry Hughes and big man Antawn Jamison. The

The GOAT

Michael Jordan is best known for his career with the Chicago Bulls. His two-year comeback with the Wizards is not remembered as much. But even nearing 40, Jordan was still an excellent player in Washington. He averaged 20 points per game in both seasons.

Gilbert Arenas's jersey number led to his nickname "Agent Zero."

forward had his best years with the Wizards, averaging 20 points per game. Respected for his leadership skills, Jamison served as Wizards team captain.

For a decade, point guard John Wall was the centerpiece of a promising Wizards team. He was not a monster scorer like Arenas, but Wall was still an offensive threat. Twice he averaged more than 20 points per game. But scoring took a back seat to his creative and accurate passing. Wall averaged more than 10 assists per game from 2014–15 to 2016–17. With Wall at the helm, the Wizards captured their first division title in 38 years after the 2016–17 season.

Another key piece of that 2016–17 team shared the backcourt with Wall. Shooting guard Bradley Beal was the third overall pick in 2012. Injuries hampered his first four seasons in the NBA. But by 2019–20 Beal was one of the league's best scorers. That year he averaged over 30 points per game for the first time in his career. After Wall was traded, Beal became the centerpiece of the Wizards' goals for the future.

Guard Bradley Beal made his first All-Star team during the 2017–18 season.

CHAPTER FOUR

MOMENTS OF WIZARDRY

The Chicago Packers occupy an important place in NBA history. The league opened as the Basketball Association of America (BAA) in 1946–47 with just 11 teams. Three years later, the league changed its name to the NBA. The Packers were the first attempt at NBA expansion.

The team played its first game on October 19, 1961, traveling to New York to face the Knicks. The Packers lost twice on the road before picking up their first win on October 27 at home against the St. Louis Hawks. However, defeats quickly added up over the course of that first season. Chicago won only 18 games all year.

It wasn't long before the team was on the move to Baltimore. On March 25, 1963, the Chicago club officially became the Baltimore Bullets. Less than seven months later, they played their first game of a 10-year stay in Baltimore.

Gus Johnson's 18.2 points and 17.1 rebounds per game helped push the Baltimore Bullets to the 1971 NBA Finals.

PLAYOFF THRILLS

In 1970–71 Earl "the Pearl" Monroe, Wes Unseld, and Gus Johnson were leading the way in Baltimore. By then the team was struggling to get past the New York Knicks in the playoffs. The Knicks knocked the Bullets out in 1969 and 1970. Despite falling behind 2–0 in 1971, the Bullets battled back and forced a Game 7. Baltimore silenced the crowd at Madison Square Garden with a thrilling 93–91 victory and advanced to its first NBA Finals.

By 1974–75 Hayes had added his talents to the mix. Unseld was a dominant rebounder. But Hayes gave Washington a true inside scorer. It all added up to the best record in team history at 60–22. After knocking off the defending champion Boston Celtics in the Eastern Conference finals, the Bullets were favored to win their first title. However, they lost in four straight games to the Golden State Warriors.

NBA CHAMPIONS

Just three years later, Washington reached the top. Unseld's MVP-level play in the 1978 Finals helped ensure Washington finally closed the deal. And the Bullets made it back to the Finals again the next season.

The Bullets navigated a difficult path to get there. They survived a pair of seven-game series. First up was a meeting with the Atlanta Hawks. Hayes led all players with 39 points

Forward Bobby Dandridge, *center*, was one of six Bullets to score in double digits during Game 7 of the 1978 NBA Finals.

and 15 rebounds in a 100–94 win in Game 7. That set up a conference finals date with the San Antonio Spurs.

Washington fell behind 3–1 in the series, then rallied to force Game 7. San Antonio led much of the game. The Spurs then had the Bullets down 10 in the fourth quarter. Instead of Unseld or Hayes, it was Bobby Dandridge who was the hero. The small forward scored 13 of his 37 points in the final quarter. He nailed a 15-foot jump shot with eight seconds left to give Washington the lead. San Antonio could not answer, and the Bullets' home crowd erupted in celebration of another Finals trip.

HIGH AND LOW

The 1985–86 Bullets won just 39 games, but fans did have Manute Bol to cheer for. The 7-foot-7-inch shot blocker from Sudan shattered the team's record book that year. He averaged five blocks per game and had 15 in one night against Atlanta.

The 1996–97 Bullets started out just 22–24. Coach Jim Lynam was fired, and former assistant coach Bernie Bickerstaff was brought back. The Bullets went on a 16–5 run to close the season. That included a win on the final day to make the playoffs for the first time in nine years.

Towering center Manute Bol, *left*, spent the first four seasons of his 10-year NBA career in Washington.

Gilbert Arenas, *left*, fades away for his game-winning shot against the Chicago Bulls in 2005.

BUZZER BEATERS

That 1997 playoff appearance was the last as the Bullets. It was also Washington's last postseason appearance for eight years. The Wizards made their first playoff appearance in 2004–05. That was the year of the Big Three in Washington. Their scoring leader, Gilbert Arenas, refused to let his team lose in Game 5 of the opening round against the Chicago Bulls.

Tied at 110–110 with under five seconds to play, Arenas backed into a defender. He spun to his right and drove toward the hoop. Suddenly he stopped and pulled up for a shot. It hit nothing but net as the buzzer sounded. The Wizards finished off the Bulls at home in Game 6 to win their first playoff series since 1982.

In 2016–17 the Wizards were heavy underdogs to the Boston Celtics in the playoffs. The Celtics showed up to the arena for Game 6 wearing black clothing. It was a not-so-subtle message that this was a funeral for the

Wizards guard John Wall soaks up the crowd after his dramatic three-pointer pushed the Wizards to a seventh game against the Boston Celtics in their 2017 playoffs series.

Wizards. Washington point guard John Wall took the statement personally. He had no plans to let his championship dreams die.

At home, the Wizards trailed by two with less than 10 seconds left. Wall caught the inbounds pass and squared up.

Noticing his defender was backing off, Wall drilled a deep three-pointer for the lead. A last-second try by Boston was off target, and the fans celebrated the first Game 7 for Washington since 1979.

Wall wasn't around for the next Wizards playoff appearance in 2021. It was up to Bradley Beal to lead his team there. The Wizards had to endure a play-in round just to make the playoffs. After dropping the first game against Boston, Washington's backs were against the wall. With a team-high 25 points from Beal, the Wizards destroyed the Indiana Pacers 142–115. The blowout victory secured the number eight seed in the Eastern Conference playoffs. Fans hoped this would be the first of many playoff memories from Beal and their Wizards.

TIMELINE

1961

The Washington Wizards begin life in Chicago as the Packers. The nickname lasts one year before the team is renamed the Zephyrs in 1962.

1963

The team relocates to Baltimore and becomes the Bullets.

1965

The Bullets make their first playoff appearance in team history. They win their first series by beating the St. Louis Hawks in the opening round.

1968

Baltimore drafts Wes Unseld second overall. His record-setting career lasts until 1981.

1971

Despite a regular-season record of 42–40, the Bullets advance all the way to the NBA Finals.

1973

The Bullets relocate to Landover, Maryland, just outside of Washington, DC. They spend a season as the Capital Bullets before changing their name to the Washington Bullets.

1975

Washington makes its second NBA Finals but fails to win a Finals game against the Golden State Warriors.

1978

The Bullets break through to their first NBA title with the help of an MVP performance from Unseld.

1987

The Bullets finish 42–40 and reach the playoffs. It is their last winning record for ten years.

1989

The Bullets play their first regular-season game in Baltimore since 1973.

1991

Susan O'Malley is named team president, becoming the first female president of a major American professional sports franchise.

1997

The Bullets change their name to the Wizards and adopt a new color scheme and logo. The team also opens a new arena in downtown Washington.

2005

With the help of a Gilbert Arenas buzzer beater, the Wizards win their first playoff series since 1982.

2017

Washington wins its first division title since 1979.

2020

Bradley Beal finishes the season averaging 30.5 points per game, becoming the first player in franchise history to average more than 30 points in a season since Walt Bellamy in 1961–62.

FRANCHISE HISTORY
Chicago Packers (1961–62)
Chicago Zephyrs (1962–63)
Baltimore Bullets (1963–73)
Capital Bullets (1973–74)
Washington Bullets (1974–97)
Washington Wizards
    (1997–)

NBA CHAMPIONSHIPS
1978

KEY PLAYERS
Gilbert Arenas (2003–10)
Greg Ballard (1977–85)
Bradley Beal (2012–)
Walt Bellamy (1961–65)
Elvin Hayes (1972–81)
Antawn Jamison (2004–10)
Gus Johnson (1963–72)
Earl Monroe (1967–71)
Wes Unseld (1968–81)
John Wall (2010–19)

KEY COACHES
Dick Motta (1976–80)
Gene Shue (1966–73, 1980–86)
Wes Unseld (1988–94)

HOME ARENAS
International Amphitheatre
    (1961–62)
Chicago Coliseum (1962–63)
Baltimore Civic Center
    (1963–73)
Cole Field House (1970–74)
Capital Centre (1973–97)
Capital One Arena (1997–)
    Formerly known as:
    MCI Center (1997–2006)
    Verizon Center (2006–17)

THE TALL AND SHORT OF IT

Washington has had both the two tallest players (Manute Bol and Gheorghe Muresan) and the two shortest players (Muggsy Bogues and Earl Boykins) in NBA history play for the team.

MR. POLLIN

Abe Pollin owned the Washington franchise for 46 years, the longest tenure of any NBA owner. The street outside Capital One Arena in Washington, DC, is now named for him.

ELITE COMPANY

The only player besides Wes Unseld to win both Rookie of the Year and MVP in the same season is Hall of Famer Wilt Chamberlain.

GOING HOME AGAIN

The Bullets moved out of Baltimore in 1973. But in 1989 the team started playing a few home games per year in the city. A total of 35 were played between 1989 and 1997, when the Wizards moved into their new downtown Washington, DC, arena.

GLOSSARY

assists
Passes that lead directly to baskets.

conference
A subset of teams within a sports league.

contender
A team that has a good chance at winning a championship.

double-double
Accumulating 10 or more of two certain statistics in a game.

draft
A system that allows teams to acquire new players coming into a league.

expansion teams
New teams that are added to an existing league.

franchise
A sports organization, including the top-level team and all minor league affiliates.

playmaker
A talented player who makes a lot of key plays for his or her team.

point guard
The player who directs a team's offensive attack.

rebound
To catch the ball after a shot has been missed.

BOOKS

Felix, Rebecca. *Michael Jordan*. Minneapolis, MN: Abdo Publishing, 2021.

Flynn, Brendan. *NBA Encyclopedia for Kids*. Minneapolis, MN: Abdo Publishing, 2022.

Mahoney, Brian. *GOATs of Basketball*. Minneapolis, MN: Abdo Publishing, 2021.

Ybarra, Andres. *Great Basketball Debates*. Minneapolis, MN: Abdo Publishing, 2019.

ONLINE RESOURCES

To learn more about the Washington Wizards, please visit **abdobooklinks.com** or scan this QR code. These links are routinely monitored and updated to provide the most current information available.

INDEX

ABOUT THE AUTHOR

Anthony K. Hewson is a freelance writer originally from San Diego. He and his wife now live in the San Francisco Bay Area with their two dogs.